T0179745

Magical History Tour ™

3 in 1 2
Collecting "The Crusades,"
"The Plague," and "Albert Einstein"

FABRICE ERRE
Writer

SYLVAIN SAVOIA
Artist

PAPERCUT⚡

Magical History Tour ™

3 in 1 2
Collecting "The Crusades,"
"The Plague," and "Albert Einstein"
By Fabrice Erre and Sylvain Savoia

Original series editors: Frédéric Niffle and Lewis Trondheim
Color Prep: Luc Perdriset
"The Crusades" and "Albert Einstein" Translations by Joseph Laredo
"The Plague" Translation by Nanette McGuinness
Lettering: Cromatik Ltd.

Mark McNabb — *Production*
Jordan Hillman and Ingrid Rios — *Original Editorial Interns*
Jeff Whitman — *Original Managing Editor*
Stephanie Brooks — *Editor*
Mike Marts — *Editor-in-Chief*

Papercutz was founded by Terry Nantier and Jim Salicrup.

October 2024
Printed in Malaysia
First Printing

ISBN 978-1-5458-1200-6

FABRICE ERRE   SYLVAIN SAVOIA

Magical History Tour

The Crusades and the Holy Wars

NICO

ANNIE

PAPERCUTZ

HEY, NICO! THIS IS MY ROOM. WHAT ARE YOU DOING IN HERE?

I WAS JUST LOOKING FOR A COMIC I LOANED YOU A WHILE AGO.

I'M SORRY IF I INVADED YOUR "SACRED SPACE," ANNIE...

GO AHEAD, MAKE FUN...

IN THE MIDDLE AGES, THAT KIND OF THING COULD HAVE STARTED A "HOLY WAR," YOU KNOW!

OH, YEAH?

OH, YES! THE CRUSADES WERE A 200-YEAR WAR BETWEEN CHRISTIANS AND MUSLIMS.

THEY WERE FIGHTING OVER A "SACRED SPACE"--AND THE WAR HAD MASSIVE CONSEQUENCES...

6

SO WHY COULDN'T THEY JUST LIVE QUIETLY WHERE THEY WERE? WHY DID THEY HAVE TO FIGHT?

THEY WANTED TO MOVE THE BOUNDARIES, CONQUER OTHER TERRITORIES.

SO THEY EACH PERSUADED PEOPLE TO JOIN THEM IN THE NAME OF "RELIGIOUS SOLIDARITY."

BUT YOU JUST SAID THE CHRISTIANS AND THE MUSLIMS WERE BOTH DIVIDED INTO DIFFERENT CAMPS!

YES, BUT FACED WITH A COMMON ENEMY, THEY ALL GOT TOGETHER.

IN THE 11TH CENTURY, THE TURKS ATTACKED THE BYZANTINES, WHO ASKED THE EUROPEANS FOR HELP.

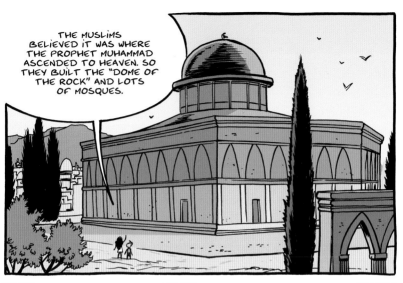

THE MUSLIMS BELIEVED IT WAS WHERE THE PROPHET MUHAMMAD ASCENDED TO HEAVEN. SO THEY BUILT THE "DOME OF THE ROCK" AND LOTS OF MOSQUES.

IT WAS ALSO A HOLY CITY FOR JEWISH PEOPLE, WHO WANTED TO PRAY AT THE "WAILING WALL," A REMNANT OF THEIR DESTROYED TEMPLE.

WOW! THAT SURE IS A LOT OF HOLINESS FOR ONE SMALL PLACE!

YES, AND EVERYONE WANTED TO BE IN CONTROL OF THIS "HOLY LAND"...

...WHICH IS WHERE THE IDEA OF "HOLY WARS" CAME FROM.

IN 1071, THE TURKS TOOK CONTROL OF JERUSALEM AND STOPPED THE CHRISTIANS FROM GOING THERE, WHICH MADE THE CHRISTIAN KNIGHTS FURIOUS. SO IN 1095, **POPE URBAN II** WENT TO CLERMONT-FERRAND IN FRANCE TO LAUNCH AN APPEAL TO ALL EUROPEANS TO GO FIGHT THE TURKISH "INFIDELS."

"CHRIST COMMANDS IT!"

TO JERUSALEM!

IT IS GOD'S WILL!

WERE THEY HAPPY TO GO ALL THAT WAY TO FIGHT?

YES, BECAUSE THE POPE PROMISED THAT ALL THEIR SINS WOULD BE FORGIVEN. IF THEY DIED, THEY'D GO STRAIGHT TO HEAVEN!

OF COURSE, KILLING AN "INFIDEL"--IN OTHER WORDS, SOMEONE WHO WASN'T A CHRISTIAN-- WASN'T CONSIDERED TO BE A SIN.

THAT'S WHAT THE "HOLY WARS" WERE ABOUT!

AND THEY THOUGHT IT WAS RIGHT FOR A POPE TO DECLARE WAR?

IN THOSE DAYS, EUROPEAN KINGS AND DUKES AND LORDS WERE ALWAYS FIGHTING, SO IT WASN'T SUCH A STRANGE IDEA.

"LET THOSE THAT ONCE WERE MERE BRIGANDS HENCEFORTH BE KNOWN AS THE KNIGHTS OF CHRIST!"

NOW I GET IT. HE GOT RID OF ALL THE CRIMINALS BY TELLING THEM THEY WERE GOING TO FIGHT FOR "JUSTICE."

KIND OF... BUT PEOPLE DIDN'T ONLY GO OUT TO JERUSALEM TO FIGHT.

THE POPE'S APPEAL WAS HEARD ALL AROUND EUROPE AND LED TO THE CREATION OF A MOVEMENT THAT LASTED 200 YEARS.

THE FIRST JOURNEY TO JERUSALEM WAS IN 1096. EVERYONE PAINTED A CROSS ON THEIR CLOTHES--SO IT BECAME KNOWN AS A "CRUSADE," FROM THE WORD "CROSS."

THERE WERE TWO PARTS TO IT: "THE PRINCES' CRUSADE," LED BY NOBLEMEN SUCH AS **GODFREY OF BOUILLON**, A DUKE FROM EASTERN FRANCE...

...AND "THE PEOPLE'S CRUSADE," LED BY A PREACHER FROM AMIENS IN NORTHERN FRANCE, WHO GATHERED ORDINARY PEOPLE AROUND HIM TO MAKE THE JOURNEY.

HIS NAME WAS **PETER THE HERMIT**.

THEY SEEM MORE... FANATICAL, RIGHT?

YES, THE PEOPLE'S CRUSADE STARTED PRETTY CHAOTICALLY, WITH LOTS OF VIOLENCE.

ON THEIR WAY TO JERUSALEM, THEY ATTACKED JEWISH PEOPLE IN GERMANY BECAUSE THEY REFUSED TO CONVERT TO CHRISTIANITY AND WERE REGARDED AS "INFIDELS."

WHEN THEY GOT THERE, THEY WERE SO DISORGANIZED THAT THE TURKS EASILY DEFEATED THEM. THOSE THAT WEREN'T KILLED WERE FORCED INTO SLAVERY.

THEY DIDN'T EXACTLY GO STRAIGHT TO HEAVEN, THEN...

THE PRINCES' CRUSADE WAS BETTER PREPARED. SUDDENLY, THE TURKS WERE FACING 100,000 SOLIDERS, BACKED BY THE BYZANTINE EMPEROR.

THE CRUSADERS TOOK SEVERAL CITIES, CLAIMING THAT GOD WAS ON THEIR SIDE. IT'S SAID THAT GODFREY OF BOUILLON SLICED A TURK IN HALF WITH A SINGLE SWIPE OF HIS SWORD!

CONSTANTINOPLE

NICEA

EDESSA

ANTIOCH

JERUSALEM

REALLY?

LET'S JUST SAY IT WAS MAINLY A CASE OF THE CRUSADERS HAVING BETTER ARMOR.

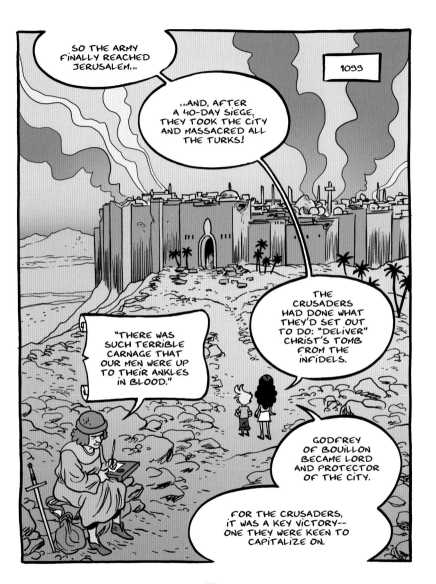

15

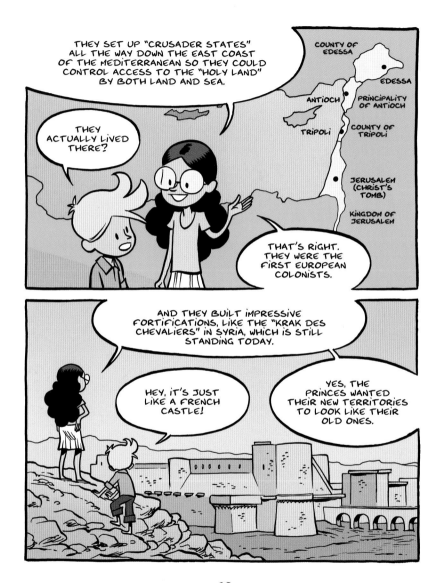

AND WERE THEY WATCHED OVER BY GUARDIAN ANGELS?

HAHA! NOT EXACTLY, BUT SOMETHING LIKE THAT.

LOOK, THOSE ARE FIGHTING MONKS. THEY BELONGED TO RELIGIOUS ORDERS AND WERE CALLED KNIGHTS TEMPLAR AND HOSPITALLER. THEY DEFENDED THE SHRINES AND THE PILGRIMS WHO VISITED THEM.

I THOUGHT MONKS DID NOTHING BUT PRAY...

WELL, THESE MONKS PRAYED **AND** FOUGHT! THEY BECAME VERY POWERFUL.

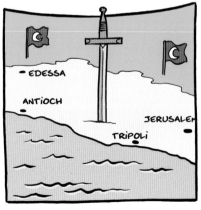

SO THE CRUSADE SEEMED TO HAVE BEEN A SUCCESS. THE CHRISTIANS HAD DEFEATED THE MUSLIMS. BUT THEIR VICTORY WAS FAR FROM SECURE...

EDESSA

ANTIOCH

JERUSALEM

TRIPOLI

IN 1144, THE MUSLIMS RECAPTURED THE CITY OF EDESSA, AND A MONK FROM BURGUNDY CALLED **BERNARD** STARTED SAYING THERE SHOULD BE A SECOND CRUSADE... AND LOTS OF PEOPLE AGREED.

MORE THAN 200,000 PEOPLE TOOK PART IN IT--THIS TIME LED BY A KING AND AN EMPEROR: **LOUIS VII** OF FRANCE AND **CONRAD III** OF GERMANY.

"TAKE THIS CROSS: THE MATERIAL ITSELF IS WORTH LITTLE, BUT THE SIGN IS WORTH NO LESS THAN THE KINGDOM OF GOD!"

EVEN MORE PEOPLE TOOK PART THAN IN THE FIRST ONE.

THE SUCCESS OF THAT CRUSADE WAS ENOUGH TO PERSUADE THEM TO CONTINUE THE "HOLY WAR."

BUT THIS TIME, IT WAS A DISASTER. OVER THE NEXT TWO YEARS (1147-1149) THE CRUSADERS WERE DEFEATED MANY TIMES AND FAILED TO RECAPTURE EDESSA.

THE LEADERS THEMSELVES FOUGHT. CONRAD III ARGUED WITH THE BYZANTINE EMPEROR, WHO REFUSED TO HELP...

...WHILE LOUIS VII, AFTER BEING BEATEN BY THE TURKS, MADE HIS PILGRIMAGE TO JERUSALEM AND THEN WENT BACK TO PARIS.

AND SO THE CRUSADERS CAME HOME EMPTY-HANDED. WELL, THEY DID BRING BACK A NEW TYPE OF FRUIT: PLUMS...

...WHICH IS WHY WHEN THE FRENCH LOSE, THEY STILL SAY, "WE FOUGHT FOR PLUMS."

MEANWHILE, THE MUSLIMS WERE BUILDING UP THEIR ARMY IN ORDER TO TAKE BACK THEIR LAND.

TO MAKE A KIND OF "RETURN CRUSADE"...

YOU COULD SAY THAT.

THE COUNTER-INVASION WAS LED BY **SALADIN**, THE SULTAN OF EGYPT AND SYRIA, WHO HAD MANAGED TO BRING MOST OF THE MUSLIMS TOGETHER.

HE'D DONE THAT BY USING THE MUSLIM WORD FOR HOLY WAR: "JIHAD."

THE WORD "JIHAD" REFERS TO THE "STRUGGLE" TO FOLLOW ISLAM, BUT SALADIN GAVE IT A WARLIKE MEANING: THE FIGHT AGAINST THE CRUSADERS, THE "INFIDELS."

ALLAHU AKBAR!*

WAIT! YOU MEAN BOTH SIDES CALLED THE OTHERS "INFIDELS"?!

ABSOLUTELY.

*GOD (ALLAH) IS MOST GREAT.

20

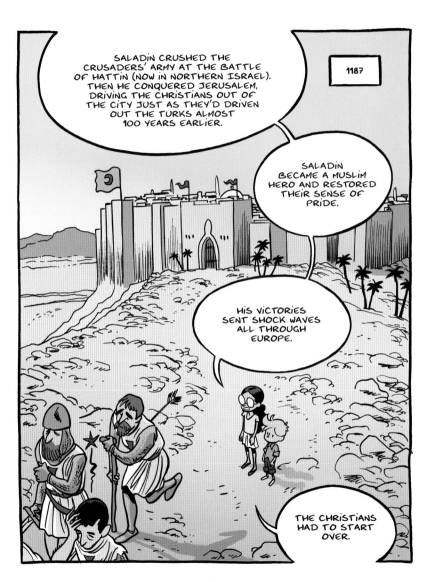

ONLY THIS TIME THEY COULDN'T CATCH THE MUSLIMS OFF GUARD.

ABSOLUTELY. THEY'D HAVE TO GET INVOLVED IN A MUCH BIGGER WAR.

IT WAS **POPE GREGORY VIII** WHO CALLED FOR A THIRD CRUSADE (1189–1192). HE SAID HUGE FORCES WOULD BE NEEDED IF JERUSALEM WAS TO BE RECAPTURED.

"THE HOLY LAND HAS BEEN SMITTEN BY THE HAND OF GOD!"

THE THREE GREAT EUROPEAN LEADERS CAME ON BOARD: **RICHARD THE LIONHEART** (ENGLAND), **FREDERICK BARBAROSSA** (GERMANY), AND **PHILIPPE AUGUSTE** (FRANCE).

THEY IMPOSED A TAX CALLED THE "SALADIN TITHE" TO PAY FOR THE CRUSADE.

BARBAROSSA WROTE TO SALADIN CHALLENGING HIM TO A DUEL.

YIKES! I BET IT WASN'T PRETTY.

BUT THE THIRD CRUSADE STARTED OUT AS BADLY AS THE SECOND. BARBAROSSA FELL INTO A RIVER AND DROWNED, SO HE NEVER HAD THE CHANCE TO FIGHT SALADIN.

NOT THE BEST WAY TO HEAVEN...

THE OTHER TWO KINGS MANAGED TO CAPTURE CYPRUS AND THE CITY OF ACRE, BUT THEY FOUGHT AMONGST THEMSELVES.

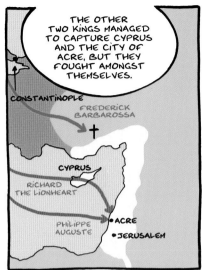

CONSTANTINOPLE

FREDERICK BARBAROSSA

CYPRUS

RICHARD THE LIONHEART

PHILIPPE AUGUSTE

ACRE

JERUSALEM

PHILIPPE AUGUSTE GOT SICK AND LOST HIS FINGERNAILS, HIS HAIR, LOTS OF SKIN, AND AN EYE. HE DECIDED TO GO BACK HOME.

RICHARD GOT SICK, TOO, BUT HE KEPT GOING... TO FACE SALADIN ALONE.

THE ENGLISH KING MANAGED TO SECURE THE CRUSADER STATES, BUT HE COULDN'T RECAPTURE JERUSALEM.

HE FOUGHT SALADIN'S ARMY SEVERAL TIMES, BUT NEVER DEFEATED THEM.

OVER THE COURSE OF THE BATTLES, THE TWO MEN BEGAN TO RESPECT EACH OTHER. WHEN RICHARD WAS INJURED, SALADIN SENT HIM HIS OWN DOCTOR!

WHY WOULD YOU HELP YOUR ENEMY?!

IT WAS ALL ABOUT CHIVALRY, YOU SEE. BRAVERY, HONOR, AND COURTESY WERE AS IMPORTANT TO MEN LIKE THAT AS THEIR RELIGIOUS BELIEFS.

IN THE END, THE TWO MEN MADE A TRUCE. THE MUSLIMS REMAINED IN CONTROL OF JERUSALEM, BUT CHRISTIAN PILGRIMS WERE ALLOWED TO ENTER THE CITY.

1192

SO THAT WAS THE END OF THE CRUSADES?

OH, NO! THEY'D GO ON FOR ANOTHER 100 YEARS.

REALLY? BUT SHOULDN'T THE TRUCE HAVE SOLVED THE WHOLE PROBLEM?

WHAT YOU MUST REMEMBER IS THAT THIS WAR WAS NO LONGER JUST ABOUT RELIGIOUS DIFFERENCES.

25

BUT I THOUGHT YOU SAID JUST NOW IT WAS A "HOLY WAR" BETWEEN CHRISTIANS AND MUSLIMS?

TO START WITH, YES, BUT THE ISSUE BECAME A LITTLE MORE COMPLICATED.

THE RIVALRIES **BETWEEN** CHRISTIANS AND **BETWEEN** MUSLIMS STARTED UP AGAIN.

SO MUCH FOR "RELIGIOUS SOLIDARITY" THEN...

SALADIN, FOR EXAMPLE, HAD SIGNED A PEACE TREATY WITH THE BYZANTINE EMPIRE, AND HE WAS GETTING WOOD AND IRON FOR HIS ARMY FROM VENICE.

THE FRIEND OF YOUR ENEMY IS A FRIEND... UH, NO...

BUT AT THE SAME TIME, A MUSLIM SECT CALLED "THE ASSASSINS" WAS THREATENING TO KILL HIM...

THE PRINCES' PRIORITY WAS TO DEFEND THEIR TERRITORY, SO THEY MADE ALLIANCES AND WAGED WARS WITH THAT AIM IN MIND.

IT WAS ALL A GIGANTIC POWER STRUGGLE.

SO ALL THIS TALK OF "HOLY WARS" WAS JUST A SMOKESCREEN?

NOT ENTIRELY. IT WAS STILL A WAY OF JUSTIFYING THE FIGHTING AND MOTIVATING THE SOLDIERS... WELL, UP TO A POINT.

IT WAS THESE RIVALRIES THAT TURNED THE FOURTH CRUSADE (1198-1204) INTO A BATTLE BETWEEN TWO SETS OF CHRISTIANS.

YOU MEAN, THEY FOUND CHRISTIANS THAT WERE "INFIDELS"?

?

CONSTANTINOPLE

NO, THEY FOUND WEALTHY CHRISTIANS THEY COULD ROB!

IN 1198, TENS OF THOUSANDS OF KNIGHTS WANTED TO MOUNT A NEW CRUSADE. THEIR AIM WAS SAIL TO EGYPT AND LIBERATE JERUSALEM BY APPROACHING IT FROM THE SOUTH.

THE VENETIANS, WHO HAD A VAST NAVY, AGREED TO TRANSPORT THEM, BUT THE CRUSADERS DIDN'T HAVE ENOUGH MONEY TO PAY THEM...

...SO THE VENETIANS MADE THEM DO A "CRUSADE" FOR **THEM!** THEY TOOK CONTROL OF ZARA,[1] A CHRISTIAN PORT, AND THEN SAILED TO CONSTANTINOPLE,[2] THE CAPITAL OF THE BYZANTINE EMPIRE.

BUT... THAT HAS NOTHING TO DO WITH RELIGION!

NOPE...

1. NOW ZADAR IN CROATIA.

2. NOW THE CAPITAL OF TURKEY, ISTANBUL.

28

IN 1204, THE CRUSADERS RUTHLESSLY RANSACKED CONSTANTINOPLE FOR THREE DAYS AND DETHRONED THE EMPEROR.

THEY'RE KILLING CHRISTIANS!

YUP, AND THEY'RE ALSO STEALING THEIR SACRED RELICS, VALUABLE RELIGIOUS ARTIFACTS-- A PIECE OF CHRIST'S CROSS, ONE OF SAINT GEORGE'S ARMS, PART OF JOHN THE BAPTIST'S HEAD...

YUUCK!

THOSE RESPONSIBLE WERE EXCOMMUNICATED* BY THE POPE. THEY'D DEFILED THE CONCEPT OF A "CRUSADE."

SO THAT WAS THE LAST ONE?

NOT AT ALL! THE DISASTERS CONTINUED THROUGHOUT THE 13TH CENTURY.

* EJECTED FROM THE CHRISTIAN CHURCH.

THE FIFTH CRUSADE (1217–1229) STARTED WHEN THE CRUSADERS LANDED IN EGYPT AND TOOK THE PORT OF DAMIETTA, BUT THEY WERE DEFEATED BY THE SULTAN...*

...AND HAD TO GO HOME WITHOUT EVEN SEEING JERUSALEM!

OH, MUMMIES!

NO, BANDAGES!

THE SIXTH CRUSADE (1228–1229) WAS LED BY THE GERMAN EMPEROR **FREDERICK II**, WHO ADMIRED MUSLIM CULTURE AND HAD BEEN EXCOMMUNICATED HIMSELF!

HE WENT TO EGYPT TO HELP THE SULTAN, WHO WAS AT WAR WITH HIS OWN BROTHER.

A CRUSADER WHO'S ANTI-POPE AND WANTS TO HELP OUT A MUSLIM MONARCH?!

* A MUSLIM RULER.

31

CHRISTIANS ROBBING OTHER CHRISTIANS AND MAKING DEALS WITH MUSLIMS... IT ISN'T REALLY A "HOLY WAR" ANYMORE...

YOU'RE RIGHT. DURING THE 13TH CENTURY, "CRUSADE" BECAME A DIRTY WORD...

...BUT THE LAST TWO WERE LED BY SOMEONE MORE DEVOUT--KING LOUIS IX OF FRANCE, WHO WAS SO PIOUS* HE WAS KNOWN AS "SAINT LOUIS."

IN 1244 HE GOT SICK AND VOWED TO MAKE A CRUSADE IF HE SURVIVED.

WHEN HE RECOVERED, HE SAID IT WAS A MIRACLE AND ORANIZED THE SEVENTH CRUSADE (1248-1254).

*DEVOUTLY RELIGIOUS.

32

BUT HE WAS CAPTURED IN EGYPT AND FORCED TO PAY FOR HIS FREEDOM. HE WENT HOME BITTERLY DISAPPOINTED, BELIEVING HE'D BEEN PUNISHED BY GOD.

AFTER THAT, SAINT LOUIS INTRODUCED MORE AND MORE RELIGIOUS LAWS: BLASPHEMY WAS FORBIDDEN, JEWISH PEOPLE HAD TO CONVERT TO CHRISTIANITY... BUT HE STILL COULDN'T LET GO OF WHAT HAD HAPPENED...

SO HE MADE ANOTHER CRUSADE IN 1270. HE LANDED IN TUNISIA, WHERE HE HOPED TO CONVERT THE EMIR BEFORE GOING ON TO JERUSALEM, BUT SOON AFTER HIS ARRIVAL HE GOT SICK AND DIED.

ANOTHER "DIVINE PUNISHMENT," PERHAPS?

MORE LIKELY A CONTAGIOUS DISEASE.

AFTER SAINT LOUIS'S TWO CRUSADES, THE SULTANS OF EGYPT GRADUALLY WON BACK THE CRUSADER STATES, WHICH NO LONGER RECEIVED EUROPEAN AID.

THE CITY OF ACRE WAS THE LAST TO FALL, IN 1291.

IT WAS THE END OF THE CRUSADES AND OF A EUROPEAN PRESENCE IN THE "HOLY LAND."

ACRE

•JERUSALEM

SO TWO HUNDRED YEARS OF CRUSADES MADE LITTLE DIFFERENCE TO THE SITUATION AROUND THE MEDITERRANEAN... OTHER THAN TO MAKE THE "THREE PEOPLES" EVEN MORE SUSPICIOUS OF EACH OTHER.

THERE WERE PROPOSALS FOR MORE CRUSADES, BUT NONE OF THEM ACTUALLY CAME TO ANYTHING.

SO NO MORE "HOLY WARS" EITHER?

OH, YES, BUT IN DIFFERENT PARTS OF THE WORLD. THANKS TO THE SPANISH *"RECONQUISTA,"* CHRISTIANS TOOK OVER THE WHOLE OF EUROPE.

AS FOR THE MIDDLE EAST, THAT CONTINUED TO BE RULED BY THE MUSLIMS, WHO RETAINED JERUSALEM UNTIL THE 20TH CENTURY. TODAY, IT'S DISPUTED BY MUSLIMS AND JEWISH PEOPLE...

OH, SO NOW THERE ARE DIFFERENT RIVALRIES?

NOT EXACTLY. WHEN THERE'S A CONFLICT IN THE MIDDLE EAST, THE WORD "CRUSADE" SOMETIMES STILL COMES ONTO PEOPLE'S LIPS.

PRESIDENT **GEORGE W. BUSH** USED IT IN 2001 AFTER THE ATTACKS ON NEW YORK...

...AND SO DID HIS "ENEMY," **SADDAM HUSSEIN,** THE IRAQI PRESIDENT, WHO CLAIMED SALADIN WAS HIS IDOL!

SO PEOPLE STILL WAGE "HOLY WARS" TODAY, JUST LIKE IN THE MIDDLE AGES?

YES--OR THEY PRETEND THAT'S WHAT THEY ARE...

WELL, IN ANY CASE, I DIDN'T INTEND TO GO ON A CRUSADE TO GET MY COMIC BACK...

...SO I'LL LEAVE YOUR "HOLY LAND" IN PEACE!

[PHEW!] THAT'S 200 YEARS OF WAR WE JUST SAVED!

And there's more...

Some people who made history

Godfrey of Bouillon
(c. 1060–1100)

A descendant of Charlemagne, Godfrey of Bouillon was one of the leaders of the First Crusade. He sold his estates to raise an army and crossed Europe to reach the "Holy Land." Arriving in Jerusalem in 1099, he ordered it to be attacked and both Muslim and Jewish citizens to be massacred. He then became "Defender of the Holy Sepulchre" — in other words, ruler of the new Kingdom of Jerusalem. He died a year later, possibly poisoned by a pinecone.

Richard the Lionheart
(1157–1199)

Although he was the King of England, Richard the Lionheart spent most of his time defending his possessions in France, which he'd inherited from his mother, Eleanor of Aquitaine. He led the Third Crusade with his rival King Philippe Auguste of France, and challenged him constantly, earning the nickname "Lionheart." He returned to the East in 1192 after signing a peace treaty with Saladin, and he died while beseiging the Château de Châlus-Charbol in 1199.

Saladin
(1138–1193)

One of a large Kurdish family, Saladin succeeded his uncle as ruler of Egypt in 1169. He promptly conquered Syria and part of Iraq, bringing the Muslims together by declaring a "jihad." He stood against the Crusaders and crushed them at the Battle of Hattin in 1187, after which he retook Jerusalem. He then repelled the Third Crusade, which had set out to defeat him. Founder of the Ayyubid dynasty, Saladin is regarded as a hero by Muslims.

Baibars
(1223–1277)

A former slave who became one of the Sultan's bodyguards, Baibars eventually ruled Egypt, joining the list of Mamluk (slave) sultans. Determined to win back the territories lost to the Crusaders, he fought against Saint Louis during the Seventh Crusade and took him prisoner in 1250. After several other victories, he succeeded in taking the Krak des Chevaliers fortress in Syria in 1271, at the end of the last Crusade.

West meets East

In the Middle Ages, the Arab world in the East was in many ways more advanced than the Christian world in the West. Thanks to the Crusades, Europeans exchanged ideas and made many advances.

Eastern delights

Sugar: *During the First Crusade, Europeans came across plantations of "sweet salt" in Syria. This was sugar cane — then unknown in the West. As well as enjoying the cakes and candies that were made from it, they recognized the importance of its use in medicine.*

Sugar cane being crushed in a mill

The astrolabe: *This was a device used by Arab astrologers to determine the height of stars above the horizon. Adapting it as a tool for navigation, European explorers subsequently used it to cross the world's oceans.*

The compass: *Invented in China, the compass reached Europe in the 12th century — probably via the Middle East.*

The zero: *First used in India, the zero ("sifr" in Arabic, meaning "empty") was adopted by Europeans around 1120 thanks to the translation of a treatise written by* **al-Khwarizmi** *by the English scholar* **Adelard of Bath**, *who had lived in Syria.*

Travel and trade

The start of passenger travel:
Most pilgrims — and there were increasing numbers of them — traveled by boat. In the 13th century, 3,000 people were transported from Marseille each year by just two ships. All this boosted the economy: in 1248, **Guy de Forez** *had to pay 975 marcs to transport troops to the East — that's 530 pounds of silver!*

The cog — a supply and troop ship used by the Knights Templar

The rise of the Italian market towns:
International trade wasn't restricted by the Holy Wars. On the contrary, in the 13th century, almost half of Genoa's trade was with Syria and Egypt, while Venice developed a trading "empire" around the Mediterranean and the Black Sea that lasted 400 years.

international transfers: *Not only trade, but also the payment of ransoms to free prisoners during the Crusades increased the international circulation of money; and the banking system developed out of money-lending and the use of bills of exchange (what we now call checks).*

An Italian merchant ship

Crusader troops

Cavalry

Mounted soldiers, generally following their prince, came from all over Europe to fight the "infidels." The "Code of Chivalry" (from the French "cheval," meaning "horse") demanded bravery, especially in religious battles.

Infantry

Foot soldiers followed the cavalry and tried to disarm their opponents with a club or guisarme (a pole used for knocking men off horses). There were usually between 7 and 12 infantry for each cavalry soldier.

Knights Templar

The Knights Templar protected both pilgrims and sacred shrines. After the loss of the Crusader States, they returned to Europe, where they became so powerful that **Philip IV of France** *disbanded them in 1307.*

Turcopoles

Turcopoles were Eastern mercenaries, mostly Christian Turks, who fought for the Crusaders. The Muslims regarded them as traitors — those who were captured at Hattin by Saladin were executed.

Timeline

The Turks take Jerusalem and forbid Christian pilgrims to visit.

▼

1078

Pope Urban II's "appeal" from Clermont-Ferrand launches the First Crusade.

▼

1095

1219

1204

▲

Damietta, in Egypt, falls to the Europeans during the Fifth Crusade.

▲

Constantinople is sacked during the Fourth Crusade.

1229

1250

▲

The German Emperor, Frederick II, wins Jerusalem back during the Sixth Crusade.

▲

Saint Louis is taken prisoner during the Sixth Crusade.

The Crusaders take Jerusalem.

The Turks win back Edessa.

Bernard calls for a Second Crusade.

1099

1144

1146

1192

1187

An agreement between Saladin and Richard the Lionheart ends the Third Crusade.

The Crusaders are defeated at the Battle of Hattin by Saladin, who retakes Jerusalem.

1270

1291

Saint Louis dies of illness in Tunis during the Eighth Crusade.

Acre, last bastion of Christendom in the Holy Land, falls and the Crusades end.

45

FABRICE ERRE   SYLVAIN SAVOIA

Magical
History Tour

NICO

ANNIE

The Plague
History of a Pandemic

PAPERCUTZ

AHH! STOP IT, NICO!

OH, ANNIE! DON'T TELL ME YOU'RE SCARED OF A LITTLE BUG!

YEAH, WELL, BELIEVE IT OR NOT, THERE ARE SOME VERY DANGEROUS CREATURES AND SOME OF THEM ARE A LOT SMALLER THAN SPIDERS.

THEY CAN CAUSE SERIOUS DISEASES: WE REFER TO THEM AS "BIOHAZARDS."

LOOK, THERE'S EVEN A SYMBOL TO SHOW IT.

BIOHAZARD

THE PLAGUE IS A DISEASE THAT'S CAUSED BY A MICROSCOPIC ORGANISM. IT'S ONE OF THE BIGGEST BIOHAZARDS IN HISTORY. IT'S KILLED TENS OF MILLIONS OF VICTIMS!

49

THE DISEASE COMES FROM RODENTS (LIKE RATS) AND IS TRANSMITTED TO HUMANS BY FLEAS.

WATCH OUT, LITTLE GUY!

IT CAN TAKE THREE FORMS.

BUBONIC PLAGUE INFECTS THE LYMPH NODES IN THE BODY.

THEY SWELL UP AND BECOME "BUBOES."

ALMOST 80% OF THOSE INFECTED DIE. IN THE MIDDLE AGES, THEY CALLED IT THE "BLACK DEATH" OR THE "GREAT MORTALITY."

WHEN THE PLAGUE IS IN THE BLOOD, IT'S CALLED "SEPTICEMIC" PLAGUE. IT AFFECTS THE ORGANS AND TURNS THE LIMBS BLACK...

WHEN IT AFFECTS THE LUNGS, IT BECOMES PULMONARY PLAGUE, WHICH IS THE MOST CONTAGIOUS OF ALL...

A SICK PERSON, A "PLAGUE VICTIM," JUST HAS TO COUGH OR SPIT TO INFECT EVERYONE AROUND THEM.

NO ONE SURVIVES IT!

I'M OUT OF HERE!

HAS THE PLAGUE BEEN AROUND FOR A LONG TIME?

YES, IT'S AN ANCIENT HORROR FOR HUMAN BEINGS. THE WORD "PLAGUE," MEANS "STRIKE" OR "WOUND" IN LATIN; IT'S A GREAT CATASTROPHE.

DOCTORS, HISTORIANS, AND ZOOARCHAEOLOGISTS HAVE DONE A LOT OF RESEARCH INTO IT...

BUT IT'S HARD TO KNOW EXACTLY WHEN IT STARTED...

IN ANCIENT TIMES, OVER 1,500 YEARS AGO, THE PLAGUE WAS OFTEN CONFUSED WITH OTHER ILLNESSES THAT HAVE THE SAME SYMPTOMS.

"CONFUSED"?

YES, MEDICINE WASN'T AS ADVANCED THEN.

I'VE ALREADY HAD THE CHICKEN POX AND SOME COLDS... ARE THERE MORE DISEASES?

WELL, YES. HUNDREDS OF THEM.

WHAT?!

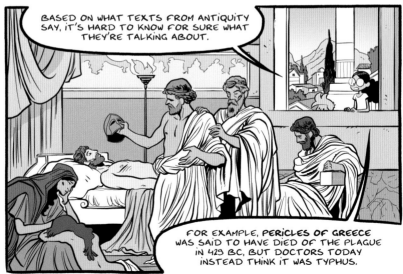

BASED ON WHAT TEXTS FROM ANTIQUITY SAY, IT'S HARD TO KNOW FOR SURE WHAT THEY'RE TALKING ABOUT.

FOR EXAMPLE, PERICLES OF GREECE WAS SAID TO HAVE DIED OF THE PLAGUE IN 429 BC, BUT DOCTORS TODAY INSTEAD THINK IT WAS TYPHUS.

IN 165 BC, THE ROMAN EMPIRE WAS HIT BY THE "ANTONINE PLAGUE," WHICH WAS DESCRIBED BY **GALEN**, A GREAT PHYSICIAN OF THE TIME. TODAY WE THINK IT WAS SMALLPOX INSTEAD.

IN THE MIDDLE AGES, THINGS HAD CHANGED: THE POPULATION HAD INCREASED AND PEOPLE TRAVELED MORE.

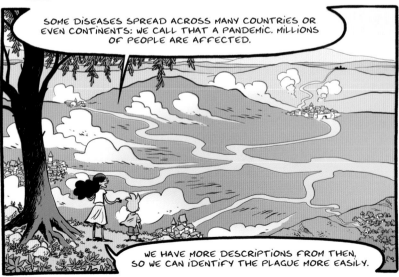

SOME DISEASES SPREAD ACROSS MANY COUNTRIES OR EVEN CONTINENTS: WE CALL THAT A PANDEMIC. MILLIONS OF PEOPLE ARE AFFECTED.

WE HAVE MORE DESCRIPTIONS FROM THEN, SO WE CAN IDENTIFY THE PLAGUE MORE EASILY.

THE FIRST PLAGUE PANDEMIC WE'RE SURE ABOUT HAPPENED IN THE 6TH CENTURY BC.

IT WAS DURING THE TIME OF **EMPEROR JUSTINIAN**, WHO RULED THE BYZANTINE EMPIRE FROM 527-565 AND CONQUERED ALMOST THE ENTIRE MEDITERRANEAN.

ATLANTIC OCEAN

BLACK SEA

CONSTANTINOPLE

CORDOBA

ROME

CARTHAGE

MEDITERRANEAN SEA

EGYPT

- ■ JUSTINIAN'S CONQUESTS
- ■ BYZANTINE EMPIRE IN 527
- ○ CAPITAL CITIES

THE "JUSTINIAN PLAGUE" APPEARED IN EGYPT IN 541.

WHAT DO YOU MEAN, IT "APPEARED?"

IT'S A MYSTERY: HISTORY DOESN'T TELL US WHERE IT CAME FROM OR WHY IT BROKE OUT WHEN IT DID.

THE PLAGUE AFFECTED THE WHOLE EMPIRE AND EVEN BEYOND. IT REACHED CONSTANTINOPLE IN 542: 20-30% OF THE CITY'S POPULATION DIED.

WERE THERE SOME PEOPLE WHO DIDN'T GET SICK?

YES, SOME PEOPLE'S BODIES ARE MORE RESISTANT THAN OTHERS. BUT THERE ARE ALSO SOCIAL AND GEOGRAPHICAL REASONS.

THE BIG CITIES WERE HIT THE HARDEST: THEY HAD MORE PEOPLE AND MORE TRADE.

GREGORY OF TOURS

HISTORY OF THE FRANKS

MARSEILLES WAS DREADFULLY DEVASTATED BY THE PLAGUE.

THAT PANDEMIC STOPPED IN 592, BUT THEN IT CAME BACK ABOUT EVERY TEN YEARS FOR THE NEXT TWO CENTURIES BEFORE COMING TO AN END.

541

592

767

THEY MANAGED TO CURE IT?

NO, ITS DISAPPEARANCE IS JUST AS MYSTERIOUS... BUT IT WASN'T PERMANENT...

14TH CENTURY

IN THE 14TH CENTURY, A SECOND PLAGUE BROKE OUT, AN EVEN BIGGER ONE: THE "BLACK DEATH"!

IT BEGAN IN CENTRAL ASIA AND AFFECTED THE MONGOL SOLDIERS IN THE "GOLDEN HORDE" IN THE 1340S.

THEY WEREN'T EXCUSED BECAUSE OF THE WAR?

IN 1347, THEY LAID SIEGE TO THE CITY OF CAFFA, ON THE BLACK SEA. BUT THEY NEVER MANAGED TO ENTER IT AND SOLDIERS DIED OF THE DISEASE.

SO THEN THE MONGOLS THREW PLAGUE-RIDDEN CORPSES OVER THE WALLS...

THE PLAGUE ENTERED CAFFA.

INFECTED ITALIAN TRADERS LEFT THE CITY AND RETURNED TO THE MEDITERRANEAN. THEY BROUGHT THE DISEASE TO SEVERAL PORTS: CONSTANTINOPLE, MESSINA, MARSEILLES...

THE ARAB PHILOSOPHER IBN KHALDUN, WHO LIVED IN TUNIS, WITNESSED IT.

A TERRIBLE PLAGUE STRUCK THE PEOPLE OF THE EAST AND THE WEST: IT TREATED NATIONS HARSHLY AND CARRIED OFF A GREAT PART OF THAT GENERATION, SWEEPING THROUGH AND WIPING OUT THE FINEST FRUITS OF CIVILIZATION.

*RAGUSA IS DUBROVNIK TODAY.

57

TRADE SPREAD IT AGAIN?

YES, IT FOLLOWED THE TRADE ROUTES ALONG THE PORTS AND RIVERS. BUT FEAR SPREAD IT, TOO.

PEOPLE FLED AND CARRIED THE DISEASE WITH THEM, TRANSMITTING IT EVERYWHERE THEY WENT.

THE AGGRESSIVENESS OF THE DISEASE WAS TERRIFYING: THE AFFLICTED DIED WITHIN SEVERAL DAYS. NO ONE KNEW HOW TO PROTECT THEMSELVES FROM IT.

ITS EFFECTS ON THE BODY WERE HORRIBLE: THE SKIN AROUND THE FLEA BITES TURNED BLACK; BOILS FILLED WITH PUS; THOSE SICK SPIT BLOOD, HALLUCINATED...

COME ON!

FROM 1347 TO 1352, AT LEAST 25 MILLION PEOPLE WERE KILLED.*

WE DON'T KNOW THE EXACT NUMBER?

NO, THERE WEREN'T PRECISE ACCOUNTS THEN.

WHOLE FAMILIES DISAPPEARED; SOMETIMES VILLAGES WERE DESERTED. SO MANY DIED THAT THE DEAD HAD TO BE BURIED TOGETHER OR BURNED.

IN PARIS, THERE WERE BETWEEN 50,000 AND 80,000 DEAD. SOME WERE REMOVED BY BOATS THAT CAME FROM THE TOWN OF CORBEIL. THAT'S WHY IN FRENCH THEY WERE CALLED "CORBILLARDS" "CORBILLARD" IN ENGLISH IS HEARSE.

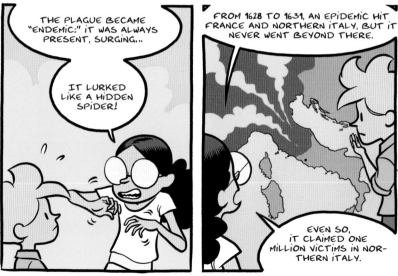

62

THERE ARE TWO AREAS WHERE THE PLAGUE RETURNED FREQUENTLY.

FOR EXAMPLE, LONDON EXPERIENCED THE PLAGUE INTERMITTENTLY FOR OVER 130 YEARS.

ALWAYS THE SAME DESOLATION...

THE LAST EPIDEMIC, FROM 1665 TO 1666, CLAIMED BETWEEN 70,000 AND 100,000 DEATHS.

DISTANT AREAS WERE INVOLVED: SEVILLE, MOSCOW, BAGHDAD... NO REGION WENT UNSCATHED.

AND THEY COULDN'T DO ANYTHING ABOUT IT?

OVER TIME, PEOPLE FOUND WAYS TO ORGANIZE THEMSELVES AND LIMIT THE SPREAD OF DISEASES.

THE KEY MEASURE WAS ISOLATION: THEY HAD TO SEPARATE OUT THE SICK PEOPLE SO AS NOT TO INFECT THE HEALTHY.

IN 1377, VENICE IMPOSED A QUARANTINE ON ALL VESSELS. THEY HAD TO STAY AT AN ISLAND OFFSHORE FOR 40 DAYS...THE AMOUNT OF TIME IT TOOK TO SEE IF THE PLAGUE WOULD BREAK OUT.

YES, LET'S GET ISOLATED!

ALL PORTS WERE EQUIPPED WITH A "LAZARETTO," AN ISOLATED BUILDING DESIGNED FOR THESE QUARANTINES.

IT KIND OF LOOKS LIKE A PRISON...

IN ORDER TO TRAVEL, BEFORE LEAVING, SHIPS HAD TO GET A "BILL OF HEALTH," WHICH CERTIFIED THERE WAS NO DISEASE ON BOARD. THEN THEY WOULD HAVE TO SHOW THE BILL AT THE PORT OF ARRIVAL.

TOWNS ISOLATED THEMSELVES. DURING THE LONDON PLAGUE IN 1665–66, THE BRITISH VILLAGE OF EYAM CHOSE TO CLOSE ITSELF AFTER DISCOVERING A CASE OF THE DISEASE.

THE TOWN LOST ROUGHLY A QUARTER OF ITS INHABITANTS, BUT THAT WAY IT AVOIDED INFECTING OTHER VILLAGES.

THAT WAS BRAVE!

IN OTHER CASES, THIS KIND OF MEASURE WAS IMPOSED ON THOSE SUFFERING FROM THE PLAGUE.

FAMILIES WERE CONFINED AT HOME, SOMETIMES BY FORCE, AS IN MILAN IN 1373.

THE HOUSES AND CLOTHING OF THOSE WHO DIED FROM THE PLAGUE WERE BURNED.

A "CORDON SANITAIRE" COULD BE ARRANGED AROUND AN INFECTED AREA: PEOPLE WEREN'T ALLOWED TO CROSS...

IF SOMEONE WHO HAD BEEN CONFINED DID ESCAPE, THEY WERE BEATEN.

Regulation

"IF THESE MEASURES WEREN'T FOLLOWED, THE EPIDEMIC COULD TURN INTO A DISASTER."

"IN MAY 1720 IN MARSEILLES, A TRADE SHIP FROM THE MIDDLE EAST ARRIVED WITH A VALUABLE CARGO OF FABRIC..."

"IT HADN'T GOTTEN ITS BILL OF HEALTH: A NUMBER OF PASSENGERS HAD DIED DURING THE CROSSING AND THE PREVIOUS PORT HAD REFUSED IT ENTRY."

THE VESSEL WAS QUARANTINED. BUT THE CITY LEADERS OF MARSEILLES WERE MERCHANTS AND THEY WANTED TO BE ABLE TO SELL THE FABRIC IN THE CARGO.

SO IT WAS UNLOADED, DESPITE THE DANGER. INFECTED FLEAS WERE HIDDEN INSIDE.

ONE MONTH AFTER THE ARRIVAL OF THE SHIP, THE PLAGUE BROKE OUT IN THE CITY.

IT PROGRESSED RAPIDLY. IN AUGUST 1720, 1,000 PEOPLE DIED EVERY DAY!

PRISONERS WERE FREED TO ACT AS "CROW-BAIT," THAT IS, TO REMOVE THE CORPSES. ALMOST ALL DIED IN TURN.

THE EPIDEMIC BEGAN TO SPREAD IN THE SOUTH OF FRANCE AND THREATENED TO BECOME A PANDEMIC.

IN SEPTEMBER, THE KING SENT TROOPS TO ISOLATE AND CONTROL THE CITY BY FORCE.

SO THE EPIDEMIC WAS BROUGHT UNDER CONTROL. AFTER ITS FINAL RETURN IN 1722, IT DIED OUT.

THIS WAS THE LAST LARGE PLAGUE EPIDEMIC IN WESTERN EUROPE (120,000 VICTIMS), COMMEMORATED IN MARSEILLES BY THIS COLUMN.

WHY DIDN'T THEY SEND DOCTORS INSTEAD OF SOLDIERS?

DOCTORS DIDN'T UNDERSTAND THE DISEASE. MEDICINE FROM THAT TIME WASN'T VERY SCIENTIFIC...

THE AIR WAS THOUGHT TO BE "PESTILENTIAL." THEY DIDN'T KNOW ABOUT GERMS, WHICH ARE TOO SMALL TO BE SEEN.

GUY DE CHAULIAC, A DOCTOR WHO OBSERVED THE ILLNESS, DISTINGUISHED BETWEEN BUBONIC AND PULMONARY PLAGUE...

BUT HE THOUGHT THE CAUSES WERE ASTROLOGICAL, THAT THE POSITIONS OF THE PLANETS CAUSED IT.

DID IT?

OH, NO, NOT AT ALL.

CHIRURGIA MAGNA

BUT WITHOUT A CORRECT DIAGNOSIS, IT WAS IMPOSSIBLE TO FIND THE RIGHT TREATMENT.

CHIRUGIA MAGNA IS LATIN FOR GREAT SURGERY.

THEY TRIED TRADITIONAL METHODS: HERBAL REMEDIES, ONION JUICE POURED ON THE BUBOES... BUT NOTHING WORKED.

STARTING IN THE 17TH CENTURY, SOME PHYSICIANS USED A LEATHER SUIT AND WORE A MASK WITH A LONG BEAK.

THEY PUT AROMATIC HERBS IN THE BEAK TO "PURIFY" THE AIR THAT HAD BEEN "FOULED" BY THE PLAGUE.

AND DID IT WORK?

NO, BUT THEIR WELL-SEALED OUTFITS ISOLATED THEM FROM THE FLEAS. SO, THEY WERE AFFECTED LESS.

IN THE FACE OF SUCH IGNORANCE, PEOPLE TURNED TOWARDS OTHER EXPLANATIONS.

SOME IMAGINED THAT EVILDOERS DELIBERATELY SPREAD THE PLAGUE.

JEWS, FEARED BY SOME CHRISTIANS, WERE ACCUSED OF POURING "VENOM AND POISONS" INTO WELLS!

ON FEBRUARY 14, 1349, BETWEEN 900 AND 2,000 JEWS WERE KILLED IN STRASBOURG. MASSACRES LIKE THIS HAPPENED THROUGHOUT ALL OF EUROPE.

THEY BLAMED LEPERS (PEOPLE AFFLICTED WITH LEPROSY) WHO LIVED APART FROM SOCIETY.

SO, WAS EVERYONE SICK BACK THEN?

THEY WERE SUSPICIOUS OF SOME OCCUPATIONS, BECAUSE THEY PROFITED FROM THE PLAGUE: NURSES, GRAVEDIGGERS...

SOME PEOPLE ALSO SEEMED AFFECTED LESS: GOATHERDS, STABLE BOYS, AND OIL BEARERS. THEIR SMELL REPELLED FLEAS, BUT NO ONE KNEW THAT YET!

IN GENEVA, IN THE SIXTEENTH AND SEVENTEENTH CENTURIES, SUPPOSED "WITCHES" WERE CALLED "PLAGUE SOWERS" AND CONDEMNED TO DEATH.

SOME PEOPLE WERE EVEN ACCUSED OF SMEARING THE PUS FROM BUBOES MIXED WITH FAT ON TOWN WALLS. THEY WERE CALLED "FATTENERS" OR "PLAGUE SPREADERS."

HEH HEH HEH

SEVERAL WERE TORTURED AND EXECUTED IN MILAN IN 1630.

ALL THESE ACCUSATIONS WERE FALSE, BUT THEY SPREAD DUE TO FEAR.

OTHERS SEARCHED FOR RELIGIOUS EXPLANATIONS. IN EUROPE DURING THE MIDDLE AGES, PEOPLE WERE CHRISTIANS AND DEEPLY RELIGIOUS...

FOR THEM, THE PLAGUE WAS CLEARLY DIVINE PUNISHMENT.

SO, THEY NEEDED TO FIND OUT WHY GOD WAS ANGRY AND MAKE AMENDS.

IN RI

DID PRAYING PROTECT THEM?

EVEN LARGE NUMBERS OF PRIESTS WERE VICTIMS OF THE DISEASE: THEY CAUGHT IT WHEN TAKING CARE OF THE DYING AND AT FUNERALS.

IN DESPAIR, SOME CHRISTIANS DECIDED TO PUNISH THEMSELVES PUBLICLY. THEY WERE CALLED "FLAGELLANTS."

THEY COULD BE RECOGNIZED BY THEIR WHIPS...

?

THEY TRAVELED IN GROUPS, GOING FROM TOWN TO TOWN, SINGING HYMNS.*

THEN THEY WOULD TAKE OFF THEIR SHIRTS AND FLOG THEMSELVES UNTIL THEY DREW BLOOD.

HUH? WHY?

CHRISTIANS BELIEVE THEY HAVE TO SUFFER TO MAKE AMENDS FOR THEIR SINS, THEIR MISTAKES...

BUT THESE FANATICS WENT EVEN FURTHER: SOME FLAGELLANTS WERE INVOLVED IN SLAUGHTERING JEWS AND REFUSED TO LISTEN TO PRIESTS...

IN 1349, POPE CLEMENT VI HAD TO FORBID PROCESSIONS LIKE THESE TO AVOID RIOTS.

*RELIGIOUS SONGS

73

SO, NOTHING MADE THE PLAGUE GO AWAY. DEATH BECAME A CONSTANT PREOCCUPATION.

PAINTERS CREATED A FRIGHTENING CHARACTER WHO THREW ARROWS AT HUMAN BEINGS, WHICH SYMBOLIZED THE DISEASE...

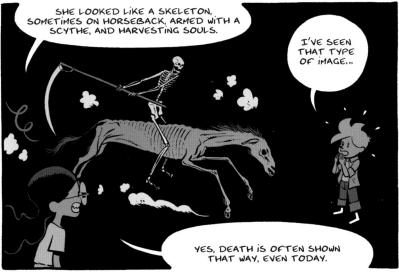

SHE LOOKED LIKE A SKELETON, SOMETIMES ON HORSEBACK, ARMED WITH A SCYTHE, AND HARVESTING SOULS.

I'VE SEEN THAT TYPE OF IMAGE...

YES, DEATH IS OFTEN SHOWN THAT WAY, EVEN TODAY.

74

IN THE 15TH CENTURY, PAINTERS STAGED "DANCES OF DEATH," WHERE THE LIVING WERE DRAGGED ALONG BY SKELETONS.

ALL SORTS OF PEOPLE WERE DEPICTED: RICH AND POOR, MEN AND WOMEN, YOUNG AND OLD...

IT WAS A WAY TO SHOW THAT DEATH WILL TAKE US ALL, NO MATTER WHO WE ARE.

SO, FOR MANY CENTURIES, PEOPLE WERE FORCED TO ACCEPT THIS DISEASE AS INEVITABLE WITHOUT REALLY UNDERSTANDING IT.

BUT THAT CHANGED COMPLETELY AT THE END OF THE 19TH CENTURY...

75

76

IN 1894, YERSIN DISCOVERED THE PLAGUE BACILLUS IN HONG KONG, A BACTERIA HE NAMED AFTER HIMSELF: YERSINIA PESTIS.

IN 1898, SIMOND FIGURED OUT THAT FLEAS TRANSMITTED THE BACILLUS.

ALL THIS... FROM A FLEA?!

THESE DISCOVERIES ALLOWED FOR A SERUM TO BE DEVISED, BUT IT WASN'T COMPLETELY EFFECTIVE. TO REDUCE INFECTIONS, THEY ALSO FOUGHT AGAINST RATS AND FLEAS.

RAT POISON

FINALLY, THE DEVELOPMENT OF ANTIBIOTICS IN THE 1930S ENABLED BETTER CARE OF THE SICK.

WE CAN FINALLY CONQUER THE PLAGUE?!

WELL, NOT COMPLETELY...

SMALLPOX IS A DISEASE THAT MEDICINE HAS ERADICATED. IT HAS DISAPPEARED AND WE THINK IT'S VIRTUALLY GONE FOR GOOD...

BUT THAT ISN'T THE CASE WITH THE PLAGUE AT ALL! IT'S VERY RESILIENT AND WE AREN'T DONE WITH BEING AFRAID OF THE "BLACK DEATH."

THE GERMS RESPONSIBLE FOR THESE DISEASES ARE KEPT IN LABS AND ACCIDENTS CAN HAPPEN.

WHY ARE WE SAVING THEM?

TO STUDY THEM AND TO CREATE "BACTERIOLOGICAL WEAPONS"...

THE JAPANESE, FOR EXAMPLE, DROPPED BOMBS ON CHINA WITH THE BUBONIC PLAGUE IN THEM FROM 1940-44.

And there's more...

People who made history...

Gökhem2
(2900 BC)

A young woman around the age of 20 who died of the plague. We don't know her name; she's identified by the site where her skeleton was found, in Gökhem, Sweden. In 2018, researchers discovered traces of the Yersinia pestis bacillus in her body's remains. She is the oldest known victim of the plague to date. This proves that the disease struck Europe very early...

Guy de Chauliac
(1298-1368)

A doctor who studied in Montpellier and Paris, France, especially, he was brought in by the pope, who lived in Avignon during this period, to treat plague sufferers and study the disease. The pope made an exception and authorized him to dissect the victims, which greatly advanced knowledge about the human body and surgery — which Guy de Chauliac specialized in. Since he was in contact with sick patients, he contracted the plague himself, but he managed to recover.

Alexandre Yersin
(1863-1943)

A doctor originally from Switzerland, he studied with **Robert Koch** *in Berlin and* **Louis Pasteur** *in France, and then practiced his trade in French colonies such as Indochina. In 1894, a plague epidemic broke out in Hong Kong: Yersin, sent to the site, secretly took samples from the cadavers and observed under the microscope a "puree of microbes," which he identified as the cause of the plague. His discovery was named* Yersinia pestis.

Albert Camus
(1913-1960)

A French writer born in Algeria, he published a novel entitled The Plague in 1947. It was inspired by the big pandemics of the past, but also by an epidemic that struck Algeria in 1944-45. Camus used the disease as a symbol; his story can be read as an allegory about the resistance that grew against Nazism, nicknamed the "Brown Plague." The book would become a literary classic.

Major Pandemics in History

The plague wasn't the only disease that spread across several continents. With the increase in the human population and globalization, other major pandemics have emerged in the past two centuries.

Cholera, *linked to a bacterium, is an intestinal disease that causes* **blue patches on the skin** *of those afflicted and kills them in two days. It's known as the "Blue Terror." Since the 19th century, it's led to seven pandemics. Appearing in India around 1817 and carried by dirty water, cholera spread in Asia and then progressively struck Russia, Europe, and finally America. In 1832 in France, it killed almost 100,000 people, among them the head of the government,* **Casimir Perier,** *who had visited some "cholera sufferers" in the hospital. The disease continues to create victims every year worldwide.*

Spanish flu, *so named because it was identified in Spain, actually developed in the U.S., beginning in March 1918. It was brought to Europe by American soldiers who came to fight in World War I.* **The second wave of the flu,** *which began in August 1918 and lasted a year, was the most deadly, causing* **at least 50 million deaths worldwide,** *many more casualties than the war itself.*

Family wearing masks to protect themselves from the flu in 1918.

AIDS, *identified in 1983, is* **a virus that attacks the human body's natural defenses.** *No longer able to fight other diseases, sufferers die as a result of this deficiency. Originally from Africa, AIDS has spread to all the continents and is* **transmitted by blood and other body fluids.** *It has led to the death of 25 million people through 2006. Since then, treatments have been developed that allow one to live with the virus, but not to get rid of it, and the AIDS pandemic isn't over.*

The **Ebola Virus** *struck West Africa from 2013-2016 and brought about the death of more than 20,000 people. The disease causes hemorrhages (blood loss) and kills over half the people it infects. Some cases were found in other continents (Spain, United Kingdom, United States...), but they were isolated rapidly and didn't lead to contagion. No treatment exists yet to overcome this disease.*

An Ebola virus particle

Corona viruses *are a family of viruses that first affect animal species, but some pass to humans and cause diseases.* **SARS,** *which appeared in China, provoked fears of a major pandemic from 2002-2004, but its impact was limited.* **COVID-19,** *which causes* **respiratory difficulties** *and was discovered in China, too, in 2019, led to a global pandemic in 2020. Unprecedented measures were adopted: many countries placed lockdowns on their inhabitants and international travel came to a halt.*

The Plague under the Microscope

For thousands of years, humans suffered from the plague without knowing what caused it: they feared the wrath of God or mysterious "miasmas." Scientific discoveries have allowed us to take a closer look at how it is transmitted.

In Ancient times, many scholars such as **Aristotle** *thought that* **diseases could be connected to tiny animals,** *but they couldn't prove this idea. It was necessary to wait until* **the end of the 16th century for the invention of the first microscopes**. *In 1609, the great astronomer* **Galileo,** *developed one.* **Athanasius Kircher,** *a German scholar who lived in Italy, used Galileo's instrument to examine the blood of victims of the 1658 Roman plague epidemic.*

In 1609, Galileo developed an "occhiolino," a microscope made up of a convex lens and concave lens.

A portrait of Athanasius Kircher in 1678.

Kircher *observed* **"little worms," invisible to the naked eye,** *which he credited with causing the disease. Kircher's observations were wrong: his instrument wasn't strong enough to see the plague bacillus, which is extremely tiny. But his conclusions were right:* **the plague is clearly caused by small organisms** *that pass from one individual to another! He suggested effective protection measures, such as isolating the sick and wearing masks.*

86

Microscope studies improved in the 17th and 18th centuries, *which permitted* the discovery of "microbes," *"little lives" that include bacteria. But scholars did not immediately understand the pathogenic role that they could play, that is, that they could cause diseases. This connection was first demonstrated in the nineteenth century by an Italian biologist,* **Agostino Bassi,** *who was studying a silkworm disease. He deduced that the principle had to be the same for other ailments, such as the plague. The discoveries then accelerated. In France,* **Louis Pasteur** *identified a number of pathogenic microorganisms and* **one of his students, Alexandre Yersin, discovered the bubonic plague's bacillus in 1894.**

The *Yersinia pestis* bacillus observed under a microscope.

The electron microscope was invented in the 20th century. *This allowed* **even smaller objects** *to be distinguished. By examining a flea on a rat, scholars then understood why it transmitted the plague: the flea has little spines that filter the blood it sucks and retain the plague bacteria. When they prick another living being (a rat or a human), these retained bacteria are injected into the veins of the victim and the plague develops!*

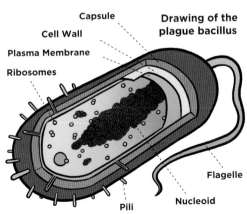

Drawing of the plague bacillus

Capsule
Cell Wall
Plasma Membrane
Ribosomes
Flagelle
Pili
Nucleoid

Timeline

First major plague pandemic, called the "Justinian Plague"

▼

541-767

Siege of Caffa by Mongolsoldiers infected with the plague

▼

1347

1720

▲

The plague returns to Marseilles. The last major epidemic in Western Europe

1665-1666

▲

Great Plague of London

1894

▲

The start of the third major pandemic in Asia. Alexandre Yersin discovers the plague bacillus.

1898

▲

Paul-Louis Simond discovers the role of fleas in plague transmission.

The plague returns to Europe and around the Mediterranean.

1348

Blamed for spreading the plague, the Jewish community in Strasbourg is massacred.

February 14, 1349

1377

Venice establishes the first quarantine measures.

1352

The plague reaches Europe from the East and halts its advance.

1920

The "ragpickers plague" infects more than 100 people in Paris

1940-1944

Japan uses bacteriological weapons containing the plague.

FABRICE ERRE   SYLVAIN SAVOIA

Magical History Tour

Albert Einstein

NICO

ANNIE

PAPERCUT Z

NOW LOOK HERE, NICO, THIS HOMEWORK JUST ISN'T GOOD ENOUGH! YOU'LL HAVE TO DO IT ALL AGAIN!

BUT, POP, SCIENCE IS WAY TOO COMPLICATED!

I JUST WANT TO GO OUT, HAVE FUN, AND DISCOVER THE WORLD!

YOU CAN DO THAT AS WELL! YOU CAN HAVE FUN, DISCOVER THE WORLD, AND EVEN **CHANGE** IT BY DOING A FEW CALCULATIONS!

THAT'S WHAT EINSTEIN DID!

HUH?

HERE HE IS. HE DOESN'T LOOK TOO SERIOUS, DOES HE?

MORE LIKE A MAD SCIENTIST!

SO THAT'S FRANK EINSTEIN?!

NO, NOT FRANK! **ALBERT** EINSTEIN!

FRANKENSTEIN WAS A MADE-UP MAD SCIENTIST WHO CREATED A MONSTER.

ALBERT WAS A REAL SCIENTIST, ONE OF THE 20TH CENTURY'S GREATEST!

BUT NOT CRAZY!

A FREE-THINKER...

...AN ACTIVIST!

ACTIVIST?

IT MEANS HE USED HIS INTELLIGENCE TO SUPPORT IMPORTANT CAUSES.

AS A PHYSICIST, HE STUDIED THE WORLD AND DESCRIBED IT IN A TOTALLY NEW WAY.

AS A PERSON, HE TRIED TO MAKE THE HUMAN WORLD A BETTER PLACE!

THERE'S SOMEONE WHO DID HIS HOMEWORK PROPERLY!

EINSTEIN LIVED AT A TIME WHEN SCIENCE WAS MAKING HUGE PROGRESS. IT WAS THE SECOND INDUSTRIAL REVOLUTION!

ELECTRICITY AND RADIO WAVES WERE INTRODUCED, CARS AND PLANES WERE INVENTED.

BUT IT WAS ALSO A PERIOD OF TERRIBLE CONFLICT--THE TWO WORLD WARS, IMPERIALISM...

YEAH, BUT SCHOOL'S NOT REALLY MY THING.

IT WASN'T HIS THING EITHER, BELIEVE ME!

OH, YEAH?!

HE DIDN'T START SPEAKING TILL HE WAS THREE, AND HE WASN'T GOOD AT FOLLOWING INSTRUCTIONS.

HE WAS VERY GOOD AT MATH, BUT NOT VERY FAST. HE'D SPEND AGES THINKING AND HE'D ASK A LOT OF QUESTIONS.

BUT HIS BIGGEST PROBLEM WAS DOING WHAT HIS TEACHERS TOLD HIM.

YOU UNDERMINE THE OTHER BOYS' RESPECT FOR ME JUST BY BEING HERE!

I SHOULD SAY THAT HE WAS BORN IN 1879 IN GERMANY, WHICH WAS RULED AT THE TIME BY A GUY NAMED **OTTO VON BISMARCK**...

...AND YOU DIDN'T MESS WITH HIM!

THAT WAS THE START OF ALBERT'S ACTIVISM--AT THE AGE OF 16. HE DIDN'T WANT TO DO HIS MILITARY SERVICE, SO HE LEFT GERMANY FOR SWITZERLAND!

I DESPISE ANY MAN WHO CAN DERIVE THE SLIGHTEST PLEASURE FROM MARCHING UP AND DOWN IN TIME WITH MUSIC!*

AND HIS PARENTS?

THEY HAD TO GO TO ITALY--THAT'S WHERE THEY WORKED. SO ALBERT TOOK THE ENTRANCE EXAM FOR THE POLYTECHNIC INSTITUTE IN ZURICH.

PIECE OF CAKE FOR A GENIUS.

YOU'RE KIDDING! HE FAILED THE FIRST TIME.

BUT HE GOT IN THE NEXT YEAR! SEE, YOU HAVE TO KEEP TRYING!

*EINSTEIN ACTUALLY SAID EVERYTHING HE SAYS IN THIS BOOK.

MILEVA GOT PREGNANT AND HAD TO GIVE UP HER STUDIES.

ALBERT GRADUATED IN 1901 AND THE FOLLOWING YEAR HE BECAME A SWISS CITIZEN, HOWEVER, HE WAS NOT ABLE TO GET A JOB AT THE UNIVERSITY.

PATENT OFFICE

TO EARN A LIVING, HE HAD TO DO AN ORDINARY OFFICE JOB.

SO HE ALMOST DIDN'T BECOME A PHYSICIST AT ALL!

THAT'S WHAT HAPPENED TO MILEVA AFTER THEY GOT MARRIED. SHE DID HELP ALBERT WITH HIS RESEARCH, BUT MOSTLY SHE HAD TO LOOK AFTER THEIR TWO CHILDREN.

EINSTEIN SPENT HIS TIME THINKING AND STUDYING MORE AND MORE DEEPLY-- AND HE REACHED SOME INCREDIBLE CONCLUSIONS!

100

101

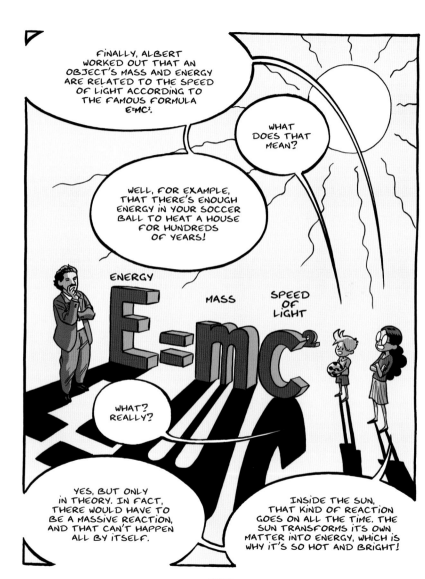

102

*IF YOU'RE INTERESTED IN MARIE CURIE, CHECK OUT MAGICAL HISTORY TOUR #13!

EINSTEIN WANTED TO GO FURTHER AND PUT TOGETHER A MORE COMPLETE THEORY, BUT IT WASN'T EASY.

HE SPENT EVEN MORE TIME WORKING, AND NEGLECTED HIS CHILDREN AND HIS WIFE, WHICH LED TO THEIR DIVORCE.

HE ALSO HAD TO LEARN ADVANCED MATH, WHICH HE HADN'T STUDIED PROPERLY WHEN HE WAS YOUNGER.

I KNOW-- ALWAYS DO YOUR HOMEWORK!

SO EINSTEIN CONTACTED AN OLD SCHOOL FRIEND, **MARCEL GROSSMANN**, WHO HAD BECOME A FAMOUS MATHEMATICIAN.

HELP ME OR I'LL GO CRAZY!

HE FILLED WHOLE NOTEBOOKS WITH EQUATIONS. IN 1912, HE WROTE THE ONE HE NEEDED, BUT HE DIDN'T REALIZE IT UNTIL 1915!

EVEN EINSTEIN COULDN'T READ HIS OWN WRITING!

BUT ALL THIS WAS JUST A THEORY. EINSTEIN ONLY **IMAGINED** AND **CALCULATED** LAWS OF PHYSICS. SOMEONE HAD TO PROVE HE WAS RIGHT.

IN 1919, HIS THEORY WAS PROVEN BY AN ASTRONOMER CALLED **EDDINGTON**, WHEN HE MADE OBSERVATIONS DURING A SOLAR ECLIPSE. OVERNIGHT, EINSTEIN BECAME A STAR!

SO HE WASN'T ECLIPSED BY ANYONE!

FROM THEN ON HE TOURED THE WORLD, GIVING LECTURES AND INTERVIEWS... IT WAS THE FIRST TIME EVER A SCIENTIST HAD BEEN INTERNATIONALLY FAMOUS.

ALMOST AS FAMOUS AS A SOCCER PLAYER!

IN 1921, HE WON THE NOBEL PRIZE--THE ULTIMATE HONOR FOR ANY SCIENTIST.

HE MET ALL KINDS OF OTHER FAMOUS PEOPLE--LIKE THE ACTOR **CHARLIE CHAPLIN.**

WHAT IMPRESSES ME MOST ABOUT YOUR ART IS ITS UNIVERSALITY. YOU DON'T SAY A WORD AND YET EVERYONE IN THE WORLD UNDERSTANDS YOU.

THAT'S TRUE, BUT YOU'RE EVEN MORE IMPRESSIVE. EVERYONE IN THE WORLD ADMIRES YOU AND YET NO ONE CAN UNDERSTAND A WORD YOU SAY.

LIKE CHAPLIN, EINSTEIN REALIZED THAT WITH CELEBRITY COMES RESPONSIBILITY, THAT HE HAD TO USE HIS FAME TO SUPPORT IMPORTANT CAUSES.

FROM 1920, HE BECAME A POLITICAL ACTIVIST!

SO HE TOOK IT UPON HIMSELF TO DENOUNCE VIOLENCE IN ALL ITS FORMS. IN 1927, HE BECAME HONORARY PRESIDENT OF THE LEAGUE AGAINST IMPERIALISM.

A YEAR LATER, HE PRESIDED OVER THE INTERNATIONAL LEAGUE FOR THE RIGHTS OF MAN, FIGHTING FOR EQUAL RIGHTS FOR EVERY HUMAN BEING.

PEACE, FREEDOM FROM OPPRESSION, HUMAN RIGHTS... EVERYONE BELIEVES IN THOSE, DON'T THEY?

YOU'D THINK SO! BUT IN THOSE DAYS, IF YOU CRITICIZED ARMIES AND COUNTRIES, YOU WERE SEEN AS A TRAITOR!

EINSTEIN VERY SOON FOUND HIMSELF IN DANGER BECAUSE OF WHAT HE'D SAID, AND ESPECIALLY BECAUSE HE WAS JEWISH.

THAT WAS WHEN ANTI-SEMITISM WAS SPREADING THROUGH GERMANY.

WHAT'S ANTI-SEMITISM?

IT MEANS HATRED OF JEWISH PEOPLE, WHO WERE ACCUSED OF HAVING CAUSED GERMANY'S DEFEAT IN 1918 AT THE END OF THE FIRST WORLD WAR.

JEWISH PEOPLE LIVING IN GERMANY?

YES, AND JEWS ALL OVER.

EINSTEIN'S FAMILY WAS JEWISH. EVEN THOUGH HE WASN'T PARTICULARLY RELIGIOUS, HE FOUND PEOPLE DESPISING HIM MORE THAN EVER BEFORE.

?   ?

REMEMBER THAT THE NAZI PARTY WAS ON THE RISE.

NO JEW CAN BE A GERMAN CITIZEN!

BUT PEOPLE SHOULD'VE BEEN PROUD THEIR COUNTRY HAD SUCH A FAMOUS SCIENTIST, RIGHT?

NOT EVERYONE WAS.

THE PHYSICIST **PHILIPP LENARD**, A NAZI SYMPATHIZER, EVEN CLAIMED THAT THE FORMULA $E=MC^2$ WASN'T EINSTEIN'S.

JUST BECAUSE HE WAS JEWISH?!

THIS SITUATION FORCED EINSTEIN TO TAKE A STAND.

THE JEWISH PEOPLE HAVE INTEGRATED INTO EUROPE (...) AND YET THEY ARE STILL REGARDED AS FOREIGNERS.

WE JEWS MUST REMIND OURSELVES THAT WE ARE AND HAVE ALWAYS BEEN A PEOPLE IN OUR OWN RIGHT.

HE'D FOUND HIMSELF A NEW KIND OF ACTIVISM...

...ZIONISM.

IS THAT ANOTHER SCIENTIFIC THEORY?

NO, NO, IT WAS A POLITICAL MOVEMENT THAT WANTED JEWISH PEOPLE TO HAVE THEIR OWN COUNTRY...

...FOR THE FIRST TIME.

IN FACT, THE BRITISH HAD PROMISED BACK IN 1917 TO HELP CREATE ONE FOR THEM IN PALESTINE, IN THE EASTERN MEDITERRANEAN.

TURKEY

DAMASCUS

IRAQ

JERUSALEM

PALESTINE

EGYPT

SAUDI ARABIA

SO EINSTEIN SUPPORTED THE FOUNDATION OF A UNIVERSITY IN JERUSALEM AS PART OF THE FIRST STEPS TO CREATING A COUNTRY.

OF JERUSALEM

THIS DOESN'T HAVE MUCH TO DO WITH RELATIVITY.

NO, BUT IT'S A VERY IMPORTANT PART OF EINSTEIN'S LIFE.

IN 1933, WHEN HITLER CAME TO POWER, ALBERT WAS TRAVELING.

HE DECIDED NOT TO RETURN TO GERMANY, WHERE HIS BOOKS WERE BURNED AND HIS HOUSE LOOTED.

AS A REFUGEE IN AMERICA HE GOT A TEACHING JOB AND TRIED TO HELP JEWISH SCIENTISTS FLEEING GERMANY TO GET INTO THE U.S.

THE RISE OF NAZISM WAS SO DANGEROUS THAT HE ABANDONED HIS PACIFIST IDEALS AND TURNED HIS ATTENTION TO IDEAS THAT WOULD HAVE TERRIBLE CONSEQUENCES.

DURING THE 1930'S, SCIENTISTS HAD MADE DISCOVERIES THAT MADE A NEW KIND OF WEAPON POSSIBLE.

RESEARCHERS HAD DISCOVERED NUCELAR FISSION--HOW TO "SPLIT" ATOMS AND RELEASE A HUGE AMOUNT OF ENERGY, JUST LIKE EINSTEIN HAD PREDICTED WITH HIS EQUATION $E=MC^2$.

ENOUGH TO HEAT A HOUSE?

OH, NO, MUCH WORSE THAN THAT.

EINSTEIN WAS AFRAID THE NAZIS WOULD WORK THIS OUT TOO, SO HE WROTE TO PRESIDENT ROOSEVELT IN 1939, JUST BEFORE THE START OF THE SECOND WORLD WAR.

This new knowledge could also lead to the development of a new type of bomb—an extremely powerful one.

EINSTEIN WAS VERY SAD THAT SCIENTIFIC PROGRESS HAD BEEN USED TO CREATE SUCH A TERRIBLE WEAPON.

The New York Times

FIRST ATOMIC BOMB DROPPED ON JAPAN

IF I'D KNOWN THAT THE GERMANS WOULD NOT SUCCEED IN MAKING A BOMB, I WOULD HAVE KEPT MY MOUTH SHUT.

FOR EINSTEIN, IT WAS A DEFEAT FOR PACIFISM.

WE'VE WON THE WAR, BUT NOT THE PEACE.

OVER THE NEXT FEW YEARS, THE U.S. AND THE U.S.S.R. MADE MANY MORE ATOMIC BOMBS. EACH ONE MORE POWERFUL THAN THE LAST, MAKING IT POSSIBLE FOR THE ENTIRE HUMAN RACE TO BE WIPED OUT.

AFTER 1945, EINSTEIN CONTINUED HIS ACTIVISM, BUT MORE BEHIND THE SCENES.

IN 1948, FOR EXAMPLE, A JEWISH NATION, ISRAEL, WAS FINALLY CREATED, BUT A WAR IMMEDIATELY STARTED BETWEEN JEWS AND ARABS.

IT WAS JUST WHAT EINSTEIN HAD FEARED. HE'D PREDICTED IT WAY BACK IN 1929.

OPEN COOPERATION WITH THE ARABS IS NECESSARY FOR PEACE AND PROSPERITY.

SO, WHEN ISRAEL'S FOUNDERS ASKED HIM TO BE PRESIDENT IN 1952, HE REFUSED.

HIS PRIORITIES WERE PACIFISM AND DEFENDING HUMAN RIGHTS, NOT JUST IN ISRAEL, BUT THROUGHOUT THE WORLD...

...AS WELL AS REMAINING INDEPENDENT!

SO HE HEADED UP THE "EMERGENCY COMMITTEE OF ATOMIC SCIENTISTS" TO PROMOTE THE PEACEFUL USE OF NUCLEAR ENERGY.

THIS MADE THE U.S. GOVERNMENT SUSPICIOUS. IT WAS THE MIDDLE OF THE COLD WAR, WHEN PACIFISM WAS CONSIDERED DANGEROUS.

THE POLICE PUT HIM UNDER SURVEILLANCE.

AND, WHEN HE STARTED DENOUNCING RACIAL SEGREGATION IN THE STATES, WHICH WAS DUE TO PREJUDICE AGAINST BLACK AMERICANS, THE HEAD OF THE FBI CALLED HIM AN "ENEMY OF THE STATE."

AFTER ESCAPING TO AMERICA BECAUSE OF HIS RELIGION, HE WAS NOW OUTLAWED BECAUSE OF HIS IDEAS.

IT SURE ISN'T EASY BEING A GENIUS...

YOU CAN SAY THAT AGAIN! EVEN IN THE SCIENTIFIC WORLD, HE FELT PRETTY ISOLATED.

SINCE 1927, SCIENTISTS HAD BEEN EXPLORING A NEW FIELD CALLED "QUANTUM PHYSICS," WHICH ALLOWED CHANCE TO MAKE THINGS HAPPEN AS WELL AS "LAWS" OF NATURE.

$$R(\lambda, T) = \dfrac{A\lambda^{-5}}{\dfrac{B}{e^{\lambda T}} - 1}$$

?

FOR EINSTEIN, THIS WAS UNTHINKABLE!

GOD DOES NOT PLAY DICE!

WHO ARE YOU, ALBERT EINSTEIN, TO TELL GOD HOW TO DO THINGS?

NEVERTHELESS, THESE IDEAS ATTRACTED A WHOLE NEW GENERATION OF PHYSICISTS.

AT THE END OF HIS LIFE, EINSTEIN WAS STILL A BIG STAR, BUT HE JUST WANTED TO BE LEFT ALONE.

THAT'S WHY HE STUCK HIS TONGUE OUT WHEN PHOTOGRAPHERS SURROUNDED HIM ON HIS WAY HOME FROM HIS 72ND BIRTHDAY PARTY!

HE DIED AT THE AGE OF 76 IN 1955.

IT WAS HEADLINE NEWS.

YORK WORLD-TELE

DR EINSTEIN IS DEAD AT 76

EVEN AFTER HIS DEATH HE WENT ON BEING TALKED ABOUT! THE DOCTOR WHO WROTE THE DEATH CERTIFICATE REMOVED HIS BRAIN FOR RESEARCH!

YUCK! AND WHAT DID HE DISCOVER?

NOT A LOT. YOU SEE, INTELLIGENCE IS MORE ABOUT HOW YOU USE YOUR BRAIN THAN ABOUT WHAT SHAPE IT IS OR HOW BIG IT IS.

And there's more...

Four other scientists who made history

Max Planck
(1858-1947)

A German physicist who came up with the idea of particles (quanta), which Einstein later developed and which eventually led to quantum physics. It was Planck's observations that gave Einstein his ideas about light. Planck won the Nobel Prize in 1918 and was an early supporter of Einstein's theories. In 1929, he and Einstein won the very first Max Planck medals!

Michele Besso
(1873-1955)

A Swiss physicist who first met Einstein when they were both at the Polytechnic Institute in Zurich and remained a close friend. Einstein's theories of relativity developed out of his long discussions with Besso, who was the only other person acknowledged in Einstein's 1905 articles. Besso also helped Albert and Mileva when they divorced, especially by looking after their children. He died in the same year as Einstein.

Karl Schwarzschild
(1873-1916)

A German astrophysicist who was fighting on the Western Front when he read Einstein's paper on general relativity in November 1915. He immediately started making complicated calculations to work out how space-time curved around a star and demonstrated that there were black holes in space. He sent his findings to Einstein, who presented them on Schwarzschild's behalf to the Prussian Academy of Sciences.

Robert Oppenheimer
(1904-1967)

An American physicist who was made scientific head of the Manhattan Project's weapons laboratory and worked on the atomic bomb. After the Second World War, he argued for the peaceful use of nuclear energy and was put under surveillance by the U.S. government. He then went back into research and served as Director of Princeton's Institute for Advanced Study, after Einstein.

Was Mileva Marić overshadowed by Einstein?

*How much credit should **Einstein's first wife** take for the development of his theories?*

*Einstein met Mileva Marić in 1896 at the Polytechnic Institute in Zurich. At that time, it was very rare for women to have access to higher education. Mileva's father had to get special permission for her to take courses normally reserved for men. She proved herself **highly gifted at both physics and math**, but became pregnant in 1900 and was unable to finish her studies, which made it difficult for her to pursue a career as a scientist.*

*Mileva and Albert married in 1903. They had three children together and for many years they lived as both **professional colleagues** and husband and wife, sharing ideas and discussing the theory of relativity. In a letter to Mileva, Albert even referred to it as "our theory."*

But Mileva was restricted by convention, which expected her to be a housewife, and was never able to pursue a career as a researcher. Only Albert's name appeared on the articles that were published.

The marriage ended in divorce in 1919 and their relationship became strained. Albert distanced himself from her and even from their children, and **he would never acknowledge the part she claimed to have played** *during their years of study and research.*

So what was Mileva's contribution to Einstein's discoveries? **The question is still hotly debated.** *For some, the fact that Albert continued to publish articles after their separation, while Mileva did not, proves that she was not involved in the development of the theories of relativity. For others, Mileva simply suffered the fate of many women at that time—to be forced to live and work in the shadow of men, without ever being given due recognition.*

Einstein and astronomy
Eddington's observations

In May 1919, the English astrophysicist **Arthur Eddington** *sailed to the islands of São Tomé and Principe, off the coast of Africa, to observe an eclipse of the sun. When the sun disappeared behind the moon, he saw that stars near to the sun appeared to be out of position relative to the Earth.* **The light the stars emitted was deflected by the mass of the sun.** *It proved that Einstein was right: space-time curved around a large mass.*

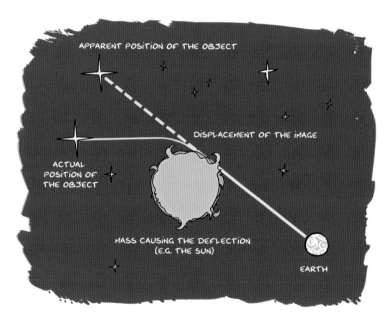

APPARENT POSITION OF THE OBJECT

DISPLACEMENT OF THE IMAGE

ACTUAL POSITION OF THE OBJECT

MASS CAUSING THE DEFLECTION (E.G. THE SUN)

EARTH

This phenomenon has been observed many times since. It is called "gravitational lensing" and it means that stars are not always where you think they are!

Hubble's discovery

In 1929, the American astrophysicist **Edwin Hubble** *argued that the universe is expanding—* **the galaxies are getting farther and farther apart***. Einstein rejected this idea. He was convinced the universe was constant. Yet his own theories showed that it was expanding. So he tried to come up with formulas that would prove the theory wrong. He couldn't. Eventually, Einstein accepted the idea, and admitted that rejecting it had been "the stupidest mistake I ever made."*

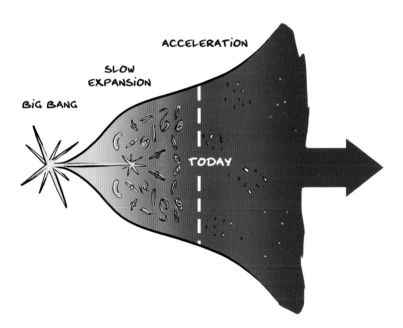

Hubble's discovery eventually led to the **Big Bang** *theory, according to which the universe started expanding 13.7 billion years ago.*

What use are Einstein's theories?

They tell you where you are

GPS satellites that send the signals to our cars so we know where we are travel very fast through space as they orbit the Earth—which means that time passes more slowly for a satellite than it does for us, as Einstein predicted. So their built-in clocks have to be constantly adjusted for them to give us the right information.

They make electric gates work

The "photoelectric effect" discovered by Einstein in 1905, which won him the 1921 Nobel Prize, means that light can generate an electric current. When we break the beam of light emitted by a gate, it opens automatically.

They generate electricity

Nuclear power stations work according to Einstein's famous formula, $E=mc^2$. When uranium is "burned," it releases a huge amount of heat, which can be used to generate electricity. But the process must be carefully controlled, or it could be disastrous!

They help you to earn money (sometimes)

Decisions on how to invest in the stock market are based on Einstein's theory of "Brownian motion." But the laws of economics are not quite as precise as the laws of physics, which means that things don't always work out as they should. That's why there was a financial crash in 2008!

Timeline

Born in Ulm (Germany) on March 14th.

▼

1879

Admitted to the Polytechnic Institute in Zurich (Switzerland).

▼

1896

1933

▲

Leaves Germany for good when Hitler comes to power.

1928

▲

Becomes President of the International League for the Rights of Man.

1939

▲

Writes to Franklin D. Roosevelt warning him of the danger of nuclear fission.

1948

▲

Publishes his book _The World as I See It._